History of America

AMERICA ENTERS THE
INDUSTRIAL REVOLUTION

Written by Susan Hamen

Rourke
Educational Media

rourkeeducationalmedia.com

*Scan for Related Titles
and Teacher Resources*

www.rourkeeducationalmedia.com

PHOTO CREDITS:
Photo credits: North Wind Picture Archives, cover; Shutterstock Images, cover, 5, 11, 17, 25, 31, 37; North Wind Picture Archives/Photolibrary, 4, 6, 10, 12, 13 (right), 16, 18, 23 (top), 24, 28 (right), 35 (right), 36, 41, 43 (third from top), 44 (top), 45 (top); The Print Collector/Photolibrary, 7, 19, 43 (second from bottom), 44 (bottom); Dorling Kindersley, 9, 13 (left); Chris Forsey/Dorling Kindersley, 14; Library of Congress, 21 (top), 21 (bottom), 28 (left), 33 (left), 33 (right), 35 (left), 39 (right), 40, 42 (top), 42 (second from bottom), 42 (bottom), 43 (top), 43 (second from top), 43 (bottom); Lewis Wickes Hine/Library of Congress, 23 (bottom); Joseph D. Barnell/Photolibrary, 26; C. M. Bell/Library of Congress, 29; Antique Research Centre/Photolibrary, 30, 42 (second from top), 45 (bottom); Nancy Carter/North Wind Picture; Archives/ Photolibrary, 32; National Motor Museum/Photolibrary, 39 (left)

Edited by Jill Sherman

Cover design by Nicola Stratford, bdpublishing.com

Interior layout by Tara Raymo

Library of Congress PCN Data

Hamen, Susan
 America Enters the Industrial Revolution / Susan Hamen.
 ISBN 978-1-62169-827-2 (hard cover)
 ISBN 978-1-62169-722-0 (soft cover)
 ISBN 978-1-62169-931-6 (e-Book)
 Library of Congress Control Number: 2013936295

Also Available as:

Rourke Educational Media
Printed in the United States of America,
North Mankato, Minnesota

Table of Contents

Chapter 1

Slater's Spinning Mill

Samuel Slater was a young **textile** mill manager from Derbyshire, England. In 1789 he disguised himself as a farmer and secretly boarded a boat and left for the United States. He sailed from London to New York, where he hoped to use his skills and knowledge.

Britain did not want other countries to learn British technology. Men such as Slater knew that their knowledge would be very valuable in other parts of the world. In North America, few people knew how to build and operate such **machinery**.

Slater hoped to make his fortune helping build a U.S. textile **industry**. He had been an **apprentice** to a man who built machinery for textile mills. He had learned everything about constructing and operating this machinery. He had even memorized how to build the mills on which he had worked.

Samuel Slater's textile mill in Pawtucket, Rhode Island, was the first built in the United States.

When Slater arrived in New York, he began working for a factory. He built parts for spinning jennies, which were large spinning wheels that produced yarn. Soon, he saw a newspaper advertisement for a different job. Two Rhode Island men were seeking someone who could run yarn-spinning equipment. Slater contacted the men, William Almy and Moses Brown. The three soon became partners.

Samuel Slater
(1768–1835)

Samuel Slater learned about textile mills in Great Britain before coming to the United States.

THE FIRST MILL

Until the 1790s Great Britain was the only place in the world where yarn was spun using water-powered mills. That changed when Samuel Slater built the first U.S. cotton mill in Pawtucket, Rhode Island, in 1790. By 1849, there were more than 123,000 mills and factories in the United States.

The spinning jenny reduced the amount of work needed to produce yarn, with a worker able to work eight or more spools at once. As technology advanced, as many as 120 spools could be worked at once.

Slater started building a water-powered cotton mill on the Blackstone River in Pawtucket, Rhode Island. Working from memory, he built a spinning mill like the one he worked on in England.

In late 1790 the mill was up and running. At first, workers walked on a treadmill to create the power to run the mill. The mill **carded** and spun cotton into thread. The thread was shipped to local weavers. The weavers then wove the thread into cloth. Soon the **waterwheel** was in place. Now the river could power the mill.

Slater's cotton mill was one of the inventions that sparked the U.S. Industrial Revolution. Before this, many goods

were produced by hand at home. Now these goods were manufactured in factories by machines, on a much larger scale.

Waterwheels were used in grain, wood, and textile mills.

CHILD LABOR

In the first year after the mill opened, Slater hired nine children between the ages of 7 and 12. They worked 12 hours per day during the winter and between 14 and 16 hours during the summer months. Within the next few years, Slater had employed dozens of children.

Slater's mill was only the beginning. Millions of people soon witnessed **inventions** that greatly improved their lives. Inventions such as railroads, better farm equipment, the lightbulb, the telephone, and the automobile would forever change the way people lived. The Industrial Revolution brought changes that made people's lives easier and made many tasks quicker. Life for millions of people would never be the same.

Textile mills such as this one had different types of machinery on each floor. Waterwheels powered the machines.

Before the Industrial Revolution, many people produced their own cloth and other goods at home.

Chapter 2
Pioneering the Industrial Revolution

Before 1700, most people in Great Britain lived on farms. They grew most of their own food and built their own furniture. They also made their own soap and candles at home. All work was done by hand. Children helped their parents with these chores.

Cloth manufacturing was the first industry in Great Britain that was changed forever by the Industrial Revolution. Until the 1700s English weavers made cloth by carding wool from sheep, spinning the wool into yarn, and then weaving the yarn into woolen fabric.

In the 1700s, it was discovered that whale oil could be used in candle making. While the scent was nothing to behold, the candles burned longer providing light at night.

THE MIDDLE CLASS

In Great Britain in the 1700s, the people who lived in cities and earned wages were becoming a middle class. In earlier times, there had been only wealthy landowners and poor farmers and workers. The new middle class bought luxury goods that only the upper class had been able to afford in the past. Therefore more factories were needed to produce more goods.

Ships sailing from India and the American colonies brought raw cotton to Britain. Merchants delivered it to farm families.

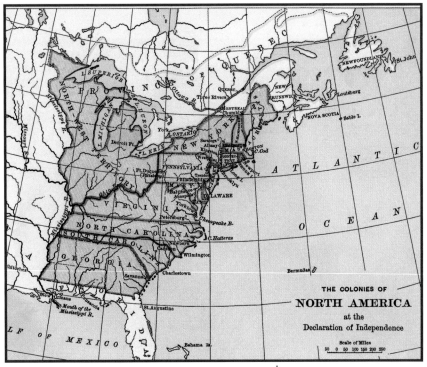

Great Britain held a lot of land in North America. The areas in pink became the United States after the Revolutionary War (1775–1783).

As textile machines became larger in size, cloth production moved into factories.

A traditional spinning wheel could only spin one spindle of thread at a time.

The families would spin and weave part-time in their homes for extra money. Women carded most of the cotton. They spun it into thread using a spinning wheel. The men then wove the thread into cotton fabric on a loom. But the demand for cotton was increasing. Spinning and weaving cotton by hand took too much time. Self employed farm families could not keep up with the booming demand for cotton products.

John Kay's 1733 invention of the flying shuttle revolutionized the textile industry. The flying shuttle did just that, it made weaving by hand fly! Weavers could race through cloth production faster than ever before.

To help with this process, James Hargreaves invented the spinning jenny in the mid 1760s. The spinning jenny could spin up to 16 spindles of thread at once. Spinners could work faster than ever before. The flying shuttle, the spinning jenny, and other inventions made Britain a dominate force in the textile industry.

Hargreaves did not apply for a patent for his Spinning Jenny until 1770 and therefore others copied his ideas without paying him any money.

Soon the demand for textiles was so great, they needed newer, larger machines. Factories began to spring up in England. These new machines were powered by waterwheels, so they were housed in factories near rivers. The increased production meant that Great Britain could **export** the extra cloth to countries all around the world. And since Great Britain ruled colonies all over the world, it could import raw materials at very low costs. Great Britain's status as a world superpower grew because of profits made from this exchange.

Inventors and crafts people saw how the cotton industry was growing. They soon invented new ways to speed up other industries. By 1800 Great Britain **mass-produced** many useful items, such as pottery, spoons, buttons, buckles, and teapots.

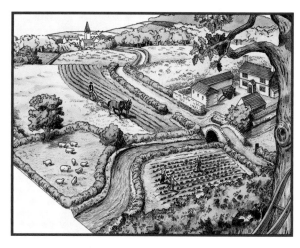

In a system of crop rotation, land that grew wheat might become a grazing pasture for sheep another year.

Farming also changed in Great Britain during the 1700s. Farmers began using crop rotation methods from the Netherlands and France. The amount of crops that a single farmer could produce increased. Since fewer farmers were needed, many left the country to work in factories. Transportation was also improving. By 1840, nearly 4,500 miles (7,200 kilometers) of **canals** crisscrossed waterways in Britain. These canals allowed farmers to ship their goods into the cities.

Not long after Great Britain's Industrial Revolution began, other European countries followed. France, Germany, and the Scandinavian countries were soon inventing and producing their own goods.

Chapter 3
A Time of Rapid Growth

Which invention reshaped the world forever? The steam engine. It became the driving force behind the new factories and mills. A British man named Thomas Newcomen invented it in 1712. This first steam engine turned water into steam, which could be used as power. Coal was burned to heat the water. In 1765 James Watt, a Scottish inventor, improved Newcomen's steam engine. Before the steam engine, factories and mills had to be located on rivers or powered by horses. The steam engine was more powerful than horses and allowed industry to move away from water sources.

Within decades, steam engines were adapted to power new and faster forms of transportation such as the steamship. In the early nineteenth century, roads did not connect most areas. Many people lived along waterways. Water was the fastest way to travel.

A steamship races a sailing ship on the Hudson River in New York in 1807.

The Erie Canal was constructed in the United States between 1817 and 1825. It joined the Great Lakes to the Atlantic Ocean. This created an important trade route for goods and materials from New York to the Great Lakes. The Erie Canal was the longest canal built at the time. Barges pulled by horses, mules, or oxen could haul up to 30 tons (27 metric tons) along the canal. Before long, other canals were dug across the United States and Britain.

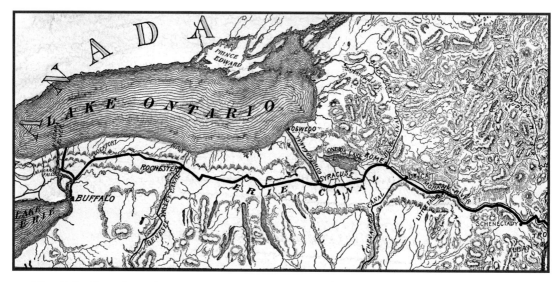

The Erie Canal made it easier to transport goods to and from the Great Lakes.

IRON INTO STEEL

In the early 1800s turning iron into steel was a long, expensive process. Steel was much stronger than iron. In 1856 Englishman Henry Bessemer discovered a way to mass-produce steel from iron ore. Machines used in factories everywhere were soon made from steel. Steel was also used to build railroads and tall buildings.

James Watt
(1736–1819)

James Watt invented an improved steam engine in 1769.

Even though Great Britain and America's economies were expanding, peace between them seemed next to impossible. From 1812 to 1815 the United States was at war with Great Britain. This war is known as the War of 1812. During this time, there was an **embargo** on British goods. The United States was no longer buying mass-produced goods from Britain.

Because of the War of 1812, the United States had to build factories of its own. Immigrants coming from European countries provided a skilled workforce. The United States was rich in natural resources such as wood, minerals, coal, and water. Factories began to spring up in the Northeast.

The U.S. Industrial Revolution started with Samuel Slater's cotton mill in Rhode Island. Then in 1793 Eli Whitney invented the cotton gin. This machine separated the cotton fibers from the seeds. Since people no longer had to do this by hand, the process of removing the seeds was much faster. Shipments of cotton from the South were sent to factories in the North. The U.S. textile industry was booming. The South began to make large profits on its cotton crops.

Francis Cabot Lowell opened the first textile mill in the United States in 1813. It performed all the tasks required to make cotton fabric from raw cotton. It was called the Boston Manufacturing Company. It was located in a tall brick mill building on a river in Waltham, Massachusetts.

Instead of hiring children to work the mill like Samuel Slater had done, Lowell hired young farm girls. Each worker performed one task in the cotton cloth production. He paid the mill girls low wages, but built them neat, clean dormitories next to the factory. Many were happy to make their own money and have respectable employment. This relationship became known as the Lowell system.

Eli Whitney (1765–1825)

Eli Whitney invented the cotton gin in 1793.

THE MILL GIRLS

The mill girls or factory girls who worked in mills such as Lowell's worked 73 hours per week. The majority of these young women were between 15 and 30 years old. They lived in dormitories next to the mill. They were expected to attend church. Older women supervised the dorms and made sure the girls followed the rules.

The cotton gin allowed workers to clean more cotton in a shorter amount of time.

By the 1830s many textile factories were in operation. The mills produced so much cloth that prices dropped. In response, factory owners began to pay their mill girls lower wages for longer working hours. The girls were pushed to work faster. Young female factory workers went on **strike** in 1834 and 1836. They wanted shorter working days and better pay.

Soon factory owners turned to immigrants to fill these positions. Entire immigrant families were willing to work at the mills for low wages. Though these families sailed to the United States from Europe to find a more promising future, many had to endure horrible working conditions.

By 1820 half of all industrial workers in the United States were children ten years old or younger. Children were needed for the jobs because their small hands could reach the small parts on factory machines. These child laborers worked ten or more hours a day and did not attend school. By the 1860s many immigrant families relied on their children for a large part of the family income.

> "There is now annually raised in the U. States. . . about one hundred millions of pounds of short staple cotton. To pick that quantity by hand . . . would require the constant labor of three hundred and thirty thousand persons. The manual labor required . . . with the aid of Whitney's gin, can now easily be performed by three hundred men. . . As a labor-saving machine, it is believed there is none, either of ancient or modern invention, which can be compared to it."
> —Niles Weekly Register, Baltimore, May 23, 1818

Francis Cabot Lowell hired young women to work in his textile mills.

Children as young as five or six years old worked in factories to help support their families.

Life for these immigrant factory families was often worse than it had been in their homelands. They lived in rundown houses in villages built by the factory owners. Working conditions in mills, factories, and mines were awful. Cotton dust filled the air and machines were loud. Workers often lost fingers or hands in factory accidents. But they took these risks in hopes of having a better life in America.

Without immigrant labor, America's explosive Industrial Revolution would not have been possible. Between 1820 and 1870, nearly 7.5 million immigrants came to the United States. Most of them were from Germany and Ireland. Another 23.5 million immigrants from all over the world flooded into the United States from 1881 to 1920. These immigrants became the workers of the Industrial Revolution.

The John Bull was an early U.S. train. It was built in Great Britain and began running in New Jersey in 1831.

Chapter 4
A Country Connected

Canals and steamboats transported resources of all types. Trees were cut down and sent to sawmills to be made into lumber for houses, shops, and factories. Iron from Michigan, Wisconsin, and Minnesota was shipped to the East Coast. Factories were producing things such as glass, paper, clocks, firearms, and metal tools. America was becoming a modern nation.

The population of the country grew throughout the 1800s. People moved farther and farther west. But it was difficult to travel where there were no rivers.

Then, in the 1820s, English inventor George Stephenson solved the travel dilemma with the invention of the steam locomotive. Through the rest of the 1800s, the network of railroads grew to connect the cities in the East, South, and Midwest. By 1863 workers had begun laying railroad track from one side of the country to the other, connecting the coasts. The Central Pacific Railroad stretched eastward from Sacramento, California. Thousands of Chinese immigrants worked to build this track. The work was backbreaking and dangerous. They used dynamite to blast tunnels through mountains.

Two years later, work on the Union Pacific Railroad began. This track stretched westward from Omaha, Nebraska. Most of the crew working on this line were Irish immigrants and men who had fought in the U.S. Civil War. They had to make their way through the Rockies and endure attacks by Native American tribes.

Large work crews laid the railroad tracks across the Great Plains. They often included large numbers of immigrant workers.

Finally, on May 10, 1869 the Central Pacific and Union Pacific railroads met at Promontory Summit, Utah. Crews had laid a total of 1,800 miles (2,900 kilometers) of new track. From New York to California, there were 3,500 miles (5,600 kilometers) of track. For the first time in the history of the United States, people could travel from the Pacific Ocean to the Atlantic Ocean by rail. By wagon, it took months to travel from coast to coast. Now a person could travel from New York City to San Francisco in a matter of days.

This was all possible thanks to the steel industry. The U.S. steel industry provided the thousands of miles of track that lay across the country. New factories built steam locomotives and railcars. Natural resources, including lumber and coal, could be transported back to the factories on the East Coast.

RAILROAD LABOR

The building of the Transcontinental Railroad was a massive construction undertaking. Both the Union Pacific and Central Pacific companies hired armies of immigrants to do the backbreaking labor of laying the rails. Central Pacific, working from the West and laying track eastward, recruited thousands of Chinese immigrants to lay track and blast tunnels through the Sierra Nevada mountains. Union Pacific, working from the opposite direction, hired European immigrants, African Americans, and Civil War veterans. Workers earned about three dollars per day.

During the nineteenth century, new inventions also improved long-distance communication. In the 1830s and 1840s, Samuel Morse perfected the telegraph. Using an electric current, the telegraph sent messages over long distances by a series of tapped codes. In May 1844 Morse sent his first message on a line that stretched from Baltimore, Maryland, to Washington, D.C. Once telegraph lines connected the coasts in the 1860s, news could travel even faster.

Telegraph lines connected the coasts by the 1860s, allowing messages to be quickly sent across the country.

Samuel Morse received a patent for his invention of the telegraph in 1847.

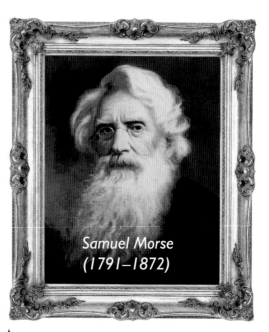

Samuel Morse
(1791–1872)

In 1876, at the age of 29, Alexander Graham Bell invented the telephone.

In 1876 Alexander Graham Bell forever changed communication with the invention of the telephone. In October of that year, Bell and his assistant Thomas Watson held the first two-way telephone conversation. The communication era had begun.

Thomas Edison created many important inventions, including the lightbulb and the phonograph.

Chapter 5
The Revolution in Full Force

Thomas Edison was one of the most brilliant inventors of all time. He changed the way people lived. He improved the telegraph and the telephone and invented the phonograph and batteries. Yet, it was his invention of the practical lightbulb in 1879 that changed the world forever.

The lightbulb was a groundbreaking invention. However, at the time of its invention, very few people had electricity, so it was useless to most people. Edison moved to New York City in 1881 and built the first electric power plant the next year.

Soon, electricity was available to the many people living in the cities. Between 1860 and 1914 the population of New York City had exploded from 850,000 to 4 million. Chicago had grown from 110,000 to 2 million people. Many of the people living in the cities were there to provide the workforce for the many industries that were growing. But they were also among the first to see many of these new technologies put to use.

As people moved to cities to work in factories, farming was changing too. Cyrus McCormick built his first horse-drawn reaper in 1831. This machine harvested grains such as wheat, hay, and oats from the field. McCormick's reaper was able to cut five times the amount of grain that a farmer could by hand. The reaper allowed U.S. farmers to grow more food. Trains and water transportation carried this food across the nation.

The invention and production of other farming tools meant fewer farmers were needed in the fields. Similar to what had happened in Great Britain, many of these workers took jobs in the steel industry, in mining, or in factories.

Cyrus McCormick's father, Robert, originally developed the idea for the reaper, but unable to get it to work properly, Cyrus took over and patented the machine in 1834.

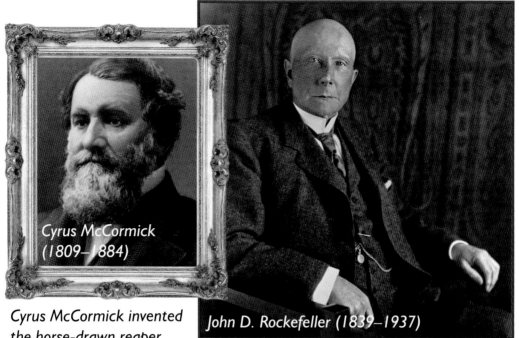

Cyrus McCormick
(1809–1884)

Cyrus McCormick invented the horse-drawn reaper.

John D. Rockefeller (1839–1937)

John D. Rockefeller was the first billionaire in the United States.

While immigrants and children were providing most of the labor for factories and railroad construction, some business owners were becoming incredibly wealthy.

John D. Rockefeller bought his first oil refinery in 1862. In 1870 he formed the Standard Oil Company. He made exclusive agreements with the railroads to transport all of his oil. In return, they lowered his shipping costs, allowing Rockefeller to sell his oil at lower rates. This arrangement drove his competitors out of business. By 1879, Standard Oil controlled 90 percent of the U.S. oil-refining industry. Rockefeller had created a **monopoly** in the oil industry. His fortune rose to over $1 billion, which would be worth at least $20 trillion today. He was the first billionaire in the United States and the wealthiest man in the world.

Andrew Carnegie worked for the railroad. He invested money in the iron industry. Eventually he owned the Carnegie Steel Company. He became a multimillionaire. Part of what made Carnegie's steel business successful was that he kept his workers' wages low. He also had very little competition. Foreign companies had to pay high taxes to export steel to the United States.

Oil and steel were not the only industries dominated by large corporations. Soon, railroads, banking, sugar, tobacco, and farm machinery were controlled by monopolies. The company leaders were known as captains of industry. They were also called robber barons because they grew rich while their workers made little money.

Underpaid workers and government officials believed it was wrong for one company to control an entire industry. The Sherman Antitrust Act of 1890 outlawed monopolies. The government broke up some of the large corporations. Yet, new large companies continued to form.

GIVING BACK

Industry leaders also used their fabulous wealth to give back to the public. Men like Carnegie and Rockefeller donated millions of dollars to public libraries, schools, music halls, and medical research institutions. Rockefeller gave away approximately $540 million during his lifetime. Carnegie helped finance hundreds of libraries across the country.

Workers went on strike in order to secure better wages and working hours. This 1892 strike at Homestead Mill ended in violence.

Andrew Carnegie (1835-1919)

Andrew Carnegie is remembered today for donating money to libraries.

"God gave me my money. I believe the power to make money is a gift from God... to be developed and used to the best of our ability for the good of mankind. Having been endowed with the gift I possess, I believe it is my duty to make money and still more money and to use the money I make for the good of my fellow man according to the dictates of my conscience."
—John D. Rockefeller

Workers formed **labor unions**. They fought for better wages and eight-hour workdays. These laborers refused to work until they were treated more fairly. Often, violence would break out. Eventually, the union workers succeeded and earned better pay and benefits.

By the late 1800s, skyscrapers were going up all over New York City. This is the view of Broadway from the top of the Singer skyscraper in 1900.

Chapter 6
Taking the Good with the Bad

Cities on the East Coast and Midwest bustled with workers and industry. The streets of New York, Boston, and Chicago were filled with carriages, trolleys, horses, and people. Vendors selling food and goods added to the traffic. In 1900 work began on the New York City subway line to help transport nearly 3.5 million residents.

The growing industries had some negative side effects. Smoke and pollution from factories filled the air and water in large cities. Wood-burning and coal-burning stoves made black smoke and soot. Families lived in cramped apartments called tenements. Stray dogs and pigs roamed the streets.

Disease was common in crowded areas. Dirty water in public wells and water pumps spread diseases, such as cholera. Many people, especially babies and young children, died from diseases caused by dirty living conditions.

Despite the hardships people in large cities were enduring, the Industrial Revolution also brought new opportunities. Shops and department stores lined the cobblestone streets. People of the middle class were able to buy nice clothing, dishes, tools, and other goods. Cities built parks for their citizens to enjoy. The cities also started building sewer systems that kept the drinking water clean.

To the amazement of millions of people, the first skyscraper was built in 1885. The Home Insurance Building in Chicago was ten stories high and had a steel frame. By the end of the nineteenth century, even taller skyscrapers were popping up in Chicago and New York City.

Household chores became easier and faster to do with the invention of the sewing machine, the electric iron, and the washing machine. Refrigerators allowed people to keep food fresh, which helped to prevent illness. Water heaters and new soaps helped with cleaning and laundry.

ANY COLOR YOU WANT

The first Model T sold for $825. Henry Ford sold more than 10,000 during the first year of production. He continued working to make his automobile even more affordable. By 1925, the Model T cost as little as $260. Ford joked, "Any customer can have a car painted any color that he wants so long as it is black."

These Model T Fords were put together on an assembly line.

Henry Ford revolutionized factories with his assembly line system.

Henry Ford (1863-1947)

Henry Ford's new production methods changed transportation forever. Ford's Model T automobile began production on October 1, 1908. Although this was not the first automobile invented, it was the first one that was affordable for most people. Ford's automobile was cheaper because he used an **assembly line** to put the cars together. Automobiles gave people of all classes the freedom of the open road.

HARPER'S WEEKLY.

JOURNAL OF CIVILIZATION.

Vol. XXVII—No. 1388.
Copyright, 1883, by Harper & Brothers. NEW YORK, SATURDAY, JULY 28, 1883. THE CENTS A COPY.
$4.00 PER YEAR, IN ADVANCE.

Immigrants and factory workers often lived in terrible conditions in tenement buildings.

The Industrial Revolution in the United States brought huge changes. Some of these changes, such as child labor, pollution, and immigrant poverty, were terrible. The upper class in the United States became incredibly wealthy and enjoyed many luxuries. Meanwhile, the lower class struggled to survive while living in filthy slums and working dangerous jobs.

GOODBYE, PIGS!

In 1842 New York City completed a sewer system that removed human and animal waste, while delivering clean water into the city.

In 1849 approximately 20,000 pigs were banished from the middle of the city.

Factories belched out soot, smoke, and other pollution, but also produced many goods that made life easier and more enjoyable.

Some of the changes brought about by the Industrial Revolution made lives easier. They helped people live longer, healthier lives. Telephones, refrigerators, cars, and even simple things such as the rubber band and safety pin were born during the Industrial Revolution. Inventions both small and large from this era forever changed the way the world lives and works.

Biographies

Many people played important roles throughout this time period. Learn more about them in the Biographies section.

Watt, James (1736–1819) - James Watt was a Scottish engineer. He improved the design of Thomas Newcomen's steam engine. In 1782, working with a partner, Watt developed and patented his new steam engine. The watt, a unit of measuring power, was named in his honor.

Whitney, Eli (1765–1825) - Eli Whitney invented the cotton gin. It separated cotton seeds from the fibers. In a single day, the cotton gin could clean as much cotton as 50 people could clean by hand. This invention helped the South become the leading cotton producer in the world.

Slater, Samuel (1768–1835) - Samuel Slater moved to the United States from Great Britain. He built the first U.S. cotton spinning mill in Pawtucket, Rhode Island. His water powered cotton mill marked the beginning of the U.S. Industrial Revolution.

Morse, Samuel (1791–1872) - Samuel Morse invented the telegraph. In May 1844, he sent his first message between Baltimore and Washington, D.C. Morse and his partners built a national telegraph network. He is also credited with Morse code, the system of dots and dashes used to send telegraphic messages.

McCormick, Cyrus (1809–1884) - Cyrus McCormick invented a horse-drawn reaping machine. His reaper could cut more than 10 acres (4 hectares) of grain per day. This revolutionized harvesting in the United States and the world. McCormick became the world's leading manufacturer of farming implements.

Carnegie, Andrew (1835–1919) - Carnegie moved from Scotland to the United States when he was a child. He went on to become a leading steel manufacturer and one of the wealthiest men of his time. Carnegie donated about $350 million of his fortune to build libraries and fund other charities.

Rockefeller, John D. (1839–1937) - John D. Rockefeller made his fortune selling oil. In 1870, he established the Standard Oil Company. By 1879, Standard Oil controlled 90 percent of U.S. oil refining. Rockefeller controlled one of the first monopolies and was labeled a robber baron. Yet, he donated about $540 million to public causes.

Edison, Thomas (1847–1931) - Thomas Edison was one of the greatest inventors of all time. Edison invented the practical lightbulb and the phonograph and improved the telegraph and telephone. He held 1,093 U.S. patents, the most any individual has ever held.

Ford, Henry (1863–1947) - Henry Ford began his career working for the Edison Illuminating Company in Detroit. He founded the Ford Motor Company. Ford reduced the cost of producing his Model T so that people could afford it. His assembly line process revolutionized factory production.

Timeline

1712
Thomas Newcomen invents the first steam engine.

1733
John Kay invents the flying shuttle.

1765
James Watt builds the first practical steam engine.

1767
James Hargreaves invents the spinning jenny.

1790
Samuel Slater opens the first cotton mill in Pawtucket, Rhode Island.

1793
Eli Whitney invents the cotton gin.

1813
Francis Cabot Lowell opens the Boston Manufacturing Company.

1825
The Erie Canal opens.

1825
Englishman George Stephenson invents the first steam locomotive.

1831
Cyrus McCormick invents the reaper.

May 24, 1844
Samuel Morse sends the first telegraph message using Morse code.

1856
Englishman Henry Bessemer designs a process to turn iron ore into steel.

May 10, 1869
The Central Pacific and Union Pacific railroads meet at Promontory Summit, Utah, connecting the continent.

1870
John D. Rockefeller forms the Standard Oil Company.

March 10, 1876
Alexander Graham Bell speaks over his invention, the telephone.

1882
Thomas Edison opens the first power station, offering electricity to New York.

October 1, 1908
Henry Ford begins producing his Model T automobile.

Reference

Key Places of the U.S. Industrial Revolution

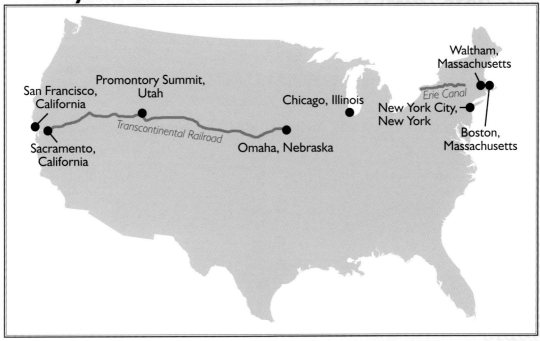

World Manufacturing, 1750-1900

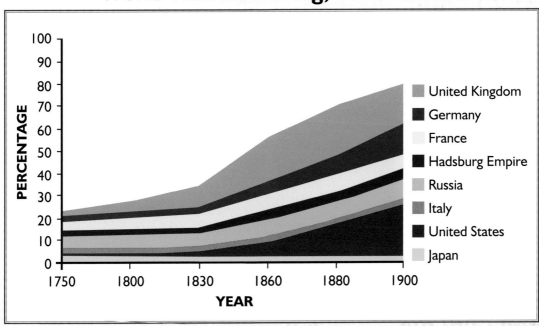

Websites to Visit

www.umassd.edu/ir

www.historylearningsite.co.uk/indrevo.htm

www.kidinfo.com/american_history/industrial_revolution.html

Show What You Know

1. How did the textile industry change with the Industrial Revolution?

2. How did farming change with the Industrial Revolution?

3. What role did the steam engine play in the Industrial Revolution?

4. How did the railroad change America?

5. Why did workers form labor unions?

Glossary

apprentice (uh-PREN-tiss): someone who is learning a skill or trade from an experienced worker

assembly line (uh-SEM-blee line): arrangement in which work passes from one station or worker to the next so that products can be quickly assembled

canals (kuh-NALZ): man-made waterways connecting bodies of water, such as lakes and rivers

carded (KARD-id): cleaned and combed fibers, such as cotton, in preparation for spinning

embargo (em-BAR-goh): a government order stopping trade with other countries

export (EK-sport): to send food or goods to other countries

industry (IN-duh-stree): the manufacturing, or making, of a particular item

labor unions (LAY-bur YOON-yuhns): organizations of workers that fight for fair wages, benefits, and safe working conditions

machinery (muh-SHEE-nuh-ree): devices that perform tasks

mass-produced (MASS pruh-DOOSD): produced in large numbers by machinery

monopoly (muh-NOP-uh-lee): an industry that is controlled by one person or company

strike (STRIKE): to refuse to work until certain demands are met

textile (TEK-stile): cloth, especially a woven cloth

waterwheel (WAW-tur-weel): a large wheel turned by running water that produces power

Index